Resurrection of Jesus

One day, in the city of Jerusalem, the king's soldiers took hold of Jesus on the judgement of Pontius Pilate, a roman senator of the time. They tore his robe, hit him with sticks and dragged him. They also pressed a crown of thorns on his head, for he had said that he was the King of Jews.

Golgotha was a place just outside the city where those who sinned were punished. Jesus was taken there. As he walked carrying the cross, a crowd of people followed him. They felt very sad for him. Jesus looked at them and said, "Do not cry for me."

Jesus was weak with all the beating. He could barely carry the cross so another person, called Simon, was made to carry it. When they reached Golgotha, the soldiers put nails through his hands and feet and hung him on the cross.

Jesus looked at them and said, “Father, forgive them, for they do not know what they are doing.”

His mother Mary and his favourite follower John, both stood there. Jesus saw his mother crying and asked John to look after her.

Suddenly, it turned very dark. Jesus was in terrible pain and he cried out to the Lord.

"Father, I place myself in your hands!" Those were Jesus's last words.

The ground shook. The temple curtain tore into two pieces. Someone said, "This man must have been the Son of God!"

Some followers lifted the body of Jesus. They washed it and wrapped it in perfumed cloth. In a garden, they placed the body inside a new tomb and covered the entrance with a big stone.

Mary and some other women cried as they watched from far.

The next day was a day of rest. The following morning, at sunrise, Mary Magdalene went to the tomb to rub a special paste on the body of Jesus. When they arrived there, they were surprised.

The stone had been rolled away. They thought that someone had stolen the body. Peter and John came quickly and went in. The tomb was empty.

A little later, Mary Magdalene went into the tomb again. This time she saw an angel and it said, “Don’t cry child, He is not here because he has risen.”

At that moment, Mary felt someone standing behind her. It was a stranger. He called her name, "Mary!" She understood. It was Jesus himself.

Jesus said, “Go and tell my disciples that I have risen”.
Mary ran to tell them, “I have seen the Lord!”